DEDICATION

To all the children of the world, to those who are struggling to survive and to those who care about that struggle.

PLAYBALL

THE MIRACLE OF CHILDREN

Ron Smothermon, M. D.

CONTEXT PUBLICATIONS
San Francisco

ISBN 0-932654-06-1

CONTENTS

ACKNOWLEDGMENTS

More than my previous books, this book is written from everyday experience. Nevertheless, certain people provided the circumstances which made my experience possible. I acknowledge Jean Smothermon whose dreams for a child came to fruition when Houston was born September 20, 1981. I acknowledge her for her courage and vision and uncompromising integrity, and most of all for the love that beats in a mother's heart.

I acknowledge Houston Smothermon who, although he can't be otherwise, is honest by nature, loving by nature, compassionate by nature, and has an inborn sense of irony and humor that showed up at four months of age. His most remarkable quality is a sense of justice and fair play I always assumed was taught to children. Apparently it isn't.

I acknowledge all fathers, whose job it is, by nature, to be visionaries for their children, to see clearly the potential of a human child, and to nurture that potential as a labor of love and joy.

I acknowledge my mother who provided a space of opportunity into which to grow so large I have never found the outer boundaries.

I acknowledge my father, who, by being absolutely tough with me, prepared me in an 18 year trial by fire to deal with the conditions of life. I didn't like him then. I love and admire him now. And, though he is gone, his life lives on in me.

Ron Smothermon, M. D.
San Francisco

PREFACE

The purpose of this book is to provide information as an opportunity for the reader to transform his or her experience of children. The domain in which we ordinarily experience children could be termed the narrative domain, that is our experience of children is determined by the circumstances and the stories we make up about them.

For many years of my life I was convinced that all children were monsters, not knowing that the monster I perceived dwelled within me. When I became a father, my eyes were opened to the truth of who children are.

Today I live with a person 38 years younger, and infinitely wiser than I, who teaches me who I am on a daily basis.

I offer you a new domain in which to experience children: the contextual domain, a domain in which children actually make a difference, independent of their circumstances, and independent of their individual stories.

Pum! Pum! Pum! go little feet and a burst of energy and light sprints into the room.

Up on Daddy's lap, certain that his company is wanted.

Big eyes looking at me, full of joy, full of mirth, full of love.

Big eyes, reflecting infinite, uncluttered space, as yet unfilled with things and thoughts of this world.

Chapter 1

TRUTH
AN INTRODUCTION

One cannot write The Truth, one can only write from The Truth. All concepts devolve to a death-like experience of life. I shall therefore spare you from concepts about children.

This book is about The Truth, and the nature of The Truth is that it cannot be stated in words. Therefore, you should be wary about a book which purports to be about The Truth. The Truth cannot be said because anything that can be said is a perception viewed from a position and is thus a part of what is, a part of the entire creation. The Truth is the entire creation, and it is impossible to view the entire creation from any particular position. The body/mind apparatus is a position. Thus viewing life from a position, anything one remarks about life based on a position is necessarily a part of The Truth, not The Truth itself. It is our fate, by virtue of having chosen to be physical, and be human, to (1) have every thought we think be a part truth, and (2) consider every thought we think as Truth. Your most sacred beliefs are only part truths and, when considered as The Truth, become lies. Even The Truth itself, when believed, becomes a lie. That is the worst news you and I will ever hear.

So, how can I propose to write a book about The Truth? The first step is contained in the paragraph above. Until one acknowledges the limitations, the limitations continue to operate as if they were actually there. Once acknowledged and given permission to be, they disappear. Until something is embraced, acknowledged, and given permission to be, it will persist as if it were real. While I can't write The Truth, and no one can, I can write *from* The Truth.

This book is about children and the porthole through which we will see children is a particular child. His given name is Houston and he was named for a courageous man of Texas history. He is here to represent all children, and any other child would grace these pages equally well. He is, in fact, here to represent human beings, the actual nature of Who People Are. I know that he is suited to the task, for through him I have discovered my own humanity.

I do not propose to write The Truth. I do propose to write from The Truth and to use the children of the world, as represented by a particular child, as my guide in writing. I propose to you that children are the light of the world and that within you exists the Spirit or Nature of the Universe which is so well represented by children. I term this Spirit the Self. It is that same Self shared by all beings.

Loud crying in the middle of the night. Wet, hungry, lonely.

A reflex takes over: up and attend to these needs, no thought, just action.

Over the shoulder, pats on the back, "Yea, yea, yea."

Back in bed, at Daddy's side this time, kiss on the cheek.

Return to infinity.

Chapter 2

MYSTERIOUS BEGINNINGS

You entered the world, streaming clouds of glory, forgetting as you came.

At exactly 12 noon September 20th, 1983, Houston entered the world as I looked on in awe. He was the 1000th baby born at Marin General Hospital that year. At the doctor's invitation, I cut the umbilical cord and held him in my arms. I was moved far beyond thought and emotion.

Taking into account certain facts, we can deduce events which occurred before we had a mind with which to remember. We are here, in physical form. We are in our bodies. Regardless of where else you may think you exist, you do exist in your body at this time. You are also "in" a certain personality, which you have developed over the course of your lifetime. Therefore, I have a question for you. How is it you exist in that body with that personality? And I suggest to you a simple answer: you chose it. If you think you did not choose it, who do you think chose it? I suggest to you that you are whoever it is you think placed you in that body. Furthermore, you are "in" a personality and I suggest that you are not that personality and that you choose that personality by creating it. If you did not chose your body and create your personality, what are you doing in there, in that body with that personality? Why isn't someone else in there instead of you? Your only other choice is to postulate the victim's position that someone else put you there. However, I suggest that you are that someone else, whoever you think that is. So, you are the responsible agent both for having your life, for having given it to yourself, and for how it is turning out. You only get to vote once about whether or not to be responsible for life and you already voted by entering the world. No more ballots from you will be counted.

It is an awesome experience to hold a newborn child in your arms and actually be in touch with Who the child is. In a way, that child's entire future flashes before you, an experience of where we all came from and where we are all going presents itself—it is an incredible burst of light in the Spirit.

In the misty, dark beginnings before the beginning, you considered the choices of remaining non-physical or becoming a human being - perhaps you lost a bet and thus became a human being. And the rules were that in becoming a human being you would forget all knowledge and give up being everything everywhere to become a particular thing in a particular place, and in that moment of choice your body was conceived and you became a human being. Although you were required to forget all knowledge, you were not required to relinquish your nature. You kept your nature, your natural identity, and brought it into the world, forgetting all else that went before. Thus you entered the world knowing all, remembering nothing, and bringing as your only possession your Self, your natural identity. You came in streaming clouds of glory, forgetting as you came.

Daddy's watch. Daddy's ring. Big prizes on a big treasure hunt through the house.

Find Daddy and give him his stuff.

Mission accomplished, on to the next adventure.

Chapter 3

BIRTH

In the beginning you were fascinated with shapes, colors, motion and sound. It made no sense then and it will never make complete sense.

After a lengthy vacation in preparation for life, during which time you dreamed dreams of former glory now unremembered, you made a long painful journey down a dark tunnel whereupon you suddenly encountered bright lights and a lot of noise. The entrance to life is as full of fright as the exit from life and in this bright light you encountered what you would later identify as human beings. However in the beginning you did not so identify them, for they were merely moving *things* against a non-moving background. If you could have focused on them, they would have seemed strange indeed, with two shiny globular things set back in their top end and a couple more objects attached to the same end on either side and the strangest thing about them was that they moved. And in your fear, something unpredictable occurred: you felt a spark of trust for these strange creatures. You brought forth trust and out of your trust your needs were fulfilled. And you forgot that you chose them to be your parents.

However your forgetting was the last thing on your mind as you became more and more fascinated with shapes, colors, and movement. You could make no sense of it whatsoever; in fact it would be years before it seemed to fall into place (and it would never fall completely into place). Nevertheless you were fascinated with it and you did your best to make it make sense. It would be months before the concepts of up and down would occur to you, and you literally did not know if you were being held with your head pointed up or down; you only noticed change in what you would later call your visual field, and a few months later you noticed that your visual field changed shape when you moved your point of view from one location to another. This provided you with many hours of entertainment.

It also provided your father with hours entertainment.

Squeals of glee, peals of laughter, running full out across the room.

Silent looks of love and knowing.

Honest, by nature, simply honest.

Hanging on Daddy's legs, riding on Daddy's hip, lying in bed and bouncing on Daddy's tummy.

When abuse becomes a pleasure you long for, you know you are a father at last.

Oh God! Why must it ever end?

Chapter 4

THE FIRST YEAR OF LIFE

In doing things you thought you could discover something about being, not knowing that doing and being exist in separate realms.

And so, through experience, you learned to be a child and you expressed yourself in your most natural state: true Self expression. When you were happy you laughed, when you were hungry, cold, or wet, you cried and screamed. You spent hours in ecstasy pressed against the flesh of those who loved you and took care of you. You spent times of agony fearing that they would never return, even when they only disappeared around a corner for a brief moment. You were presented with food and you drank and ate, knowing nothing of how to do these things — your efforts were messy to say the least. You awoke each morning not sure what you were, where you were, and it was all you could do to remember, given that you had not yet learned . . . and you forgot from whence you came.

Supposedly at the risk of "spoiling" Houston, he sleeps with with me almost every night. I know Who He Is in those hours—he is an angel and I am swept away. Often I lie awake and listen to him breathe and I am deeply moved. Houston doesn't know much in the way of ordinary, everyday information, and I would trade all I know for what he knows now.

And, through it all, you were committed to knowing, to finding out who, where, what, why, even when. Your whole life became about discovering Who You Are and thus the answer to all the other questions of life. For, while you expressed your Self perfectly, you had no notion of Who you were expressing — you were busy just expressing. Your path toward what you thought would be discovery of Who You Are led you into doing things. You thought that by doing something you could discover something about *being*. And, as your journey began, you were still *being* Who You Are, even while you were *doing* things to try to discover being. You did good things to discover being, you did bad things to discover being. You even imagined that doing could alter being and thus you began to develop a personality.

The function of a personality is to discover Who One Is and it exists in the realm of doing, while the Self exists in the realm of being. The personality is, therefore, irrelevant to discovering the Self: it neither helps nor hinders, but exists in a different realm.

Back home from a walk. Doesn't want to be back home. Screams his displeasure. Wants to be touring the neighborhood for a lifetime.

Unhappiness gives way to curiosity and soon Daddy's office is being taken apart for the 10th time in the last two days.

Giving 100% all of the time. Standing in awe of a reel-to-reel tape recorder which he has never seen before. Curiosity, burning like a fire.

Chapter 5

A BEING OF COMMITMENT

Children are beings of commitment. They are committed to the workability of life.

If you will simply observe a child, *any* child, you will discover that Who People Are is that people are Beings of Commitment. Children are limited in what they can attach their commitment to, however they are all committed — it is built into the flesh and doesn't require development. Children are committed to breathing, and thus to living. Children are committed to learning and to the mastery of life. Children are committed to others, to caring for others, to the workability of life. Selfishness must be taught by adults, for it is not inherent in human nature. Children are committed to contribution.

Houston loves to eat cookies, and as much as he loves to eat cookies, there is one thing he loves more about cookies and that is to give them away. I have seen him give his cookies away when I knew him to be hungry. And no one taught him that, it is spontaneous behavior. He will have to learn from the adults that food is supposedly scarce and not to be given away lightly.

Houston is committed to learning and this takes many forms. I have seen him create a notion that he would learn about a clock by unplugging it and dragging it across the floor *and he will not give up the idea* until he has done the deed or has himself been bodily carried away. Commitment takes many forms.

If you are concerned about the "younger generation," don't be. They are in great shape. People are born into the world with all they need to make it and with all that is needed for the world to make it. Children are naturally loving, caring and giving. So are we, and sometimes we forget our fundamental nature.

"short." We say that good times are scarce, good people are scarce, honesty is scarce, good weather is rare, and on and on. We thus put on the lens of scarcity and therefore we see life in terms of scarcity. We are *obligated* to see scarcity in life, even though it is absent, just as the world appears yellow when viewed through a yellow lens. We use the condition of scarcity to justify withholding our support from those who need it. It justifies dishonesty on our income tax forms (I know you don't want to read this), it justifies dressing in a shabby way, it justifies a nuclear buildup and the use of the threat of war to protect what there is supposedly not enough of. We risk our lives and the lives of our children to protect a myth!

INEVITABILITY

The second conditon compounds the first by postulating that what is, is itself inevitable — a veritable law of the universe. This "law of the universe" postulates "What Is Will Forever Be" (a far cry from the principle of What Is, Is). "People are the way they are, they will never change." "War is inevitable." "There has always been hunger, always will be too. Someone will always be hungry." "Into every life a little rain must fall." In fact, the condition of scarcity itself is said to be inevitable. "There will never be enough."

UNWORKABILITY

The third and final condition is the statement of something to the effect of "Whatever can go wrong, will go wrong." Life itself is postulated not to work. Given the two conditions which precede this one, unworkability is a natural outcome. However, this condition stands on its own, for if the other two disappeared, this one would persist and wreak havoc on an unsuspecting world.

There is nothing mysterious about the world of spirituality. It is simply that in life which is not physical. If you will consider that for a moment, you will realize that the spirit world is the world of thought, nothing more and nothing less. Therefore, I want to let you know who Satan is. Satan is The Condition (Scarcity, Inevitablity, and Unworkability). Out of The Condition comes all of what we think of as "evil." Satan is, therefore, an evil spiritual beingness, created of human thought, not that red demon you had in mind.

Children are born knowing nothing of The Condition. These notions are *taught*. "Growing up" means learning these things and operating one's life from them. The conditions of life are so ingrained in our cultures, they are taught by precept and example rather than by direct instruction. However, in case a child misses the point the conditions of life are hidden in many of our common everyday sayings, several examples of which are stated above. These things are taught by domination and fear. Children know better, and, in order to be loved and to get along with the big

Screams in the night, fear, and dread. Nothing will do except for Daddy to turn on the lights and tour Houston around the house.

Staring intensely at the floor over and over to see if the dreadful "it" is still there.

It isn't. Never was. Besides, Daddy is a lot bigger.

Back to the sleep of angels.

Chapter 7

INSPIRATION

Birth is an infusion of the body with spirit. Preconception, in a way, is a refresher course in aliveness and children are fresh from that course.

The conditions of life are heavy, perhaps the heaviest one is Scarcity. Even love is said to be scarce and, if the world were populated only by adults, life would be of questionable value. However, fate took pity upon us and made children, and to make room for them created the aging process and death, thus renewing us continuously with infusions of The Truth. It is as if we were called home for a refresher course from time to time. The result of that refresher course is inspiration, a filling of the body with Spirit. Children bring this quality to life and offer it to us by themselves being inspired.

Often during the day Houston will take a deep breath *and for no reason smiles* a huge grin, exhales and says "Mmmmmmmmmmmm!" and looks at me as if to say "Life is just the greatest"

Inspiration is the natural state of children. They do not need to study a religion, meditate, take a training, or anything other than be who they naturally are, and they can't avoid being that. The nature of inspiration is love and, as adults, we have difficulty appreciating the quality of love children bring to life because we view life through the conditions of life:

Scarcity, Inevitability, and Unworkability.

We experience love as if it were supposed to fit within those conditions. It is as if we wear blinders and very dark glasses to boot, thus seeing children as we are afraid we are ourselves. I have discovered the ability to remove these filters and when I do and look at Houston, I am overcome with his wisdom, compassion, love, and humanity. "Magnificence" is not an adequate word to describe him. At such times as I see him for Who He Is, the light is blinding to my eyes and my Spirit as well. The Self is blown away by its own magnificence.

Trundling into the breakfast room. Just up. Down the stairs by himself, in silence.

Steps of curious certainty up to the breakfast table.

Eyes full of peace and love and morning.

Curiosity — what's that under the table?

Clunk! Loud scream. Crying that shatters the peace of early morning. Red face, contorted in pain.

Tender young head bumped on the table's edge for the 1,062nd time.

And hurt real bad every time.

Consoled in Daddy's arms.

Chapter 8

SPIRITUALITY

The realm of thought is the first manifestation of the spirit. For all practical purposes there is no difference.

It is time to remove the shroud of mystery from the realm of spirituality. If you are a thinking being, you are a spiritual being, there is no difference. "Spirit" is that word we have to denote the fact that there are influences on the physical plane by factors present in a non-physical plane. This non-physical plane is nothing more nor less than the realm of human thought. You are not your thoughts, for you are not a thing, and your thoughts *are* the first manifestations of You to present themselves to the world. The most powerful influences on the environment are your thoughts and the thoughts of those around you. The physical world is literally given life by the spiritual world. One only need look at one's life to see the power of thoughts. You have in your life exactly what you think and expect.

Therefore, you are a spiritual being who is constantly interacting with the physical world. The choice we have, as human beings, expressing ourselves physically is the answer to the question: *What will I think?* This is the one realm in which a person has absolute dominion. No one can make you think anything or prevent you from thinking anything you like. And what you think has profound influences on your life and the lives of people around you. It literally creates life as we know it, for without your thought, life doesn't exist for you. The choice you do not have is whether or not you will think, for with the exception of rare moments, you must think, since you are a spiritual being and you are alive.

These are not issues for children, and they are taught by children just in the course of their being. Children think spontaneously and are hungry to learn more words to think with, *for thinking occurs in words, and words only, and words, unlike you, are things. By their word alone children create their world.*

Suddenly up and into Daddy's arms!

Down the stairs and into the car!

Where am I going? What are the choices?

Strapped into a safety seat and down the street.

Off to a great adventure and asleep like a log.

Chapter 9

MIND AND SELF

Children can cope with the way it is if they can find out the way it is. We adults tend to spend our time pretending about life and this is confusing for children.

Spirit or Self is inherent in human beings. It is that which creates all else, including words. It is not a thought in itself, but is that which thinks and that which listens to thoughts. It is nothing you can observe, but is that which observes. Given that the Self is unobservable, a child presents us with an opportunity to *experience* Self. The Self is experienceable only by the Self, so if you are moved by reading this book, that is Self experiencing Self.

To try to understand these matters, the Self constructs a Mind and uses the body to house the Mind. The tissues of the body are used to store memories, the major function of the Mind. The Mind then takes over for the Self and uses these memories to survive and the Self gives the Mind charge of survival. Since most situations are viewed as potentially threatening by the Self, the Mind is given the major role in expression.

The major flaw in the thinking of the Self is that it thinks it is a *part* of everything rather than everything, itself. Apparently, that is a price it pays for becoming physical. It thus conceives the possiblity of disintegration and non-existence and to protect itself allows the Mind to usurp all major areas of responsibility.

The Mind, left to its own devices, creates the beliefs which will support the notion of separation. What better beliefs and justifications than Scarcity, Inevitability and Unworkability (see Chapter 6)? Therefore, if Satan is The Condition, then all of us are possessed of Satan. These Satanic beliefs then serve as justification for evil perpetrations on other beings and finally become part of the social matrix in which we exist and through which we interpret the world.

By the way, this stuff is not "bad" or even serious, it is just what is so, and, to come to know your Self for Who You Are, it is important that you not kid your Self about it.

The problem children encounter is that adults kid themselves about it, and this is confusing for children. We pretend these things do not exist, which further ingrains them into the matrix of life. A young child wants to know the way it is and can cope with the way it is if he can only find out. The best thing we can do for our children is tell them the truth, even when it doesn't seem to be the most pleasant thing around.

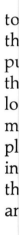

to
th
pu
th
lo
m
pl
in
th
ar

tr
th
sa
is
of
pr

D
th

then snaps them back together, looking up at me with pride and accomplishment in his expression. "Humph!" he says. Then he repeats it several times over.

Mastery requires repetition and testing. It is important to allow a child the freedom to repeat things over and over, even though we are bored to tears. Houston must become certain that the pen will behave the same each time he handles it and, therefore, someday he can use it as a tool, taking it for granted.

Children come complete with all they need to make it in life. They only need an environment which does not stop the expression of their natural learning process. We take much too much credit for our children's learning. It may be that we detract from it more than we add to it.

Standing in the middle of the room. For once at a loss for what to do.

Considering, perhaps for the first time in life. The rules. What are the rules?

Short lived consideration . . . into Daddy's wallet, flinging money and cards in all directions.

To heck with rules! Let the good times roll!

Chapter 11

PLAYING IS ALL THERE IS

*Children know life is a game and
that rules are made up. Later on
they will forget this.*

As adults, we have forgotten that all of life is a
game. We now have names (and thus concepts) for
that which is supposedly not a game. We call these
non-game games by such names as "job," "relationship," "marriage," "education," "parenthood," and so
on. These names allow us to forget that all we do in
life is a game with rules for scoring and winning, con-
sequences for losing, all played out in relationship to
other players. From time-to-time I remind people
that what they are doing is a game. "No it's not!" they
say, in a tone of voice that protests such an insult.
"This is real life!" Absolutely — real life is a set called
"game" and contains many other games as subsets.

Children are not so serious about it all — they
know life is a game containing many other games.
Houston is playing all the time, without let-up. Some
of his games are "Flirting," "Bump-A-Head," "Kiss-
ing," "Carry-me-around," "Play Bored," "Mimicing,"
"Peek-A-Boo," "Take Things Apart," and a new one,
"Running." These games are played with great joy

and enthusiasm, even the ones that require crying which can turn into gales of laughter at any moment.

One of Houston's games is "Playball," and it is my favorite because I get to play too. Houston is the proud owner of a large red, white, and blue plastic beach ball that is filled with air. The game is to get to the door and past Daddy with the ball and then throw the ball down the stairs and watch Daddy go get it. The rules read that Houston wins about half the time and that the entire game is conducted in the atmosphere of constant baby laughter. It is a miracle to behold, for the game comes out of nothing. It was not taught, it was created, and it exists for absolutely no purpose other than the game itself. It is a perfect statement of life itself, complete with the joy and enthusiasm that underlies all activity and all emotions. The joy and enthusiasm are the expression of Self, of Who One Is; the activity and emotions of life are the games which the Self is playing.

Without Spirit or Self, there is no life, and there are no games. What I am saying is that life and games are one and the same and the Spirit playing the games is You, but not the "you" you are accustomed to thinking of yourself as. Who you are used to thinking of yourself as are actually the pieces of the game itself. But you are not the pieces of the game, nor are you the whole game, rather you are the player who creates the game, the rules, and the components of the game such as the emotions (the way you "feel" about it all).

When one searches for Who One Is, one must strip away all the "things," even the things one thought were not things, such as feelings and concepts. Even a thought is a "thing" in this sense and you are not your thoughts, rather you are the thinker. However the notion "thinker" is itself a thought and thus is not Who You Are either. It is the paradox of life that one cannot see Who One Is because one is the seer, not the seen. A wonderful analogy is the human eye. It never sees itself, although it sees all else. In the same manner, you will never see Who You Are, thus your search is hopeless until you realize that you are the creator, the player, hiding from itself by virtue of the rules of its game. And that realization is itself a creation, not the creator.

Houston is not the game Playball. He is that who dreamed up the game Playball, who has no name because any name is necessarily not the creator, but rather a production of the creator. You can never catch this as long as you think of yourself as a thing. Play Ball is the creation of a true God.

Nor is his name Houston — that is a word we attached to his body for convenience. Who You Are doesn't have a name, for if it did, then it would no longer be Who You Are. That is the trouble with the word "God," for once having given it a name, we think we are a step closer to knowing who that is and actually we are a step back. And as we go on to define

God, with each definition we are one step further removed from knowing God. Finally God becomes a thing in our minds so far from Who God Is, we may as well give up, quit thinking about it, and go back to brushing our teeth. So, the word "God" has had grave damage done to it, perhaps irreparable damage. The same process occurs with any substitute word we apply for God. Some people, in search for God, make vows of silence and some go for years and do not utter a word.

So here is the low-down on God: God is the first one who said "Play Ball!" Your local theologian will not necessarily agree, but he or she is, like you and me, too smart to know better.

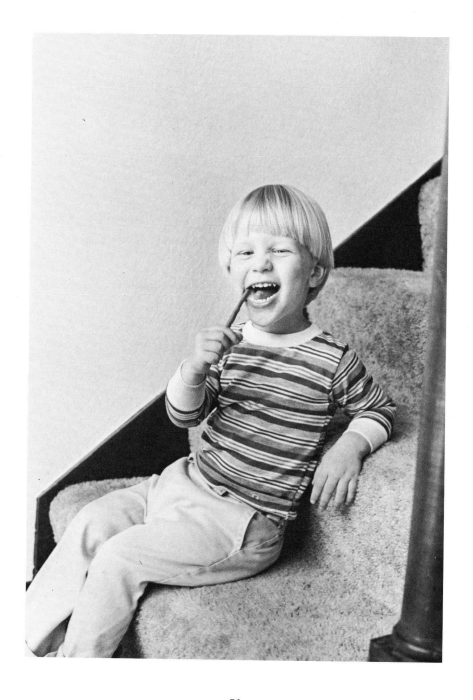

A cavity! Already a cavity! Appointment with the dentist next Thursday. Must start brushing young new teeth.

Grabbing for the toothbrush. Wants to brush his teeth, likes the taste of toothpaste.

"Teeeeeeth!" he says with glee.

Daddy does it, so it must be the thing to do. Imitating, already imitating.

Isn't this all going by rather fast?

Chapter 12

THE ABSOLUTENESS OF LOVE

*Compassion is living in the being-
ness of all beings. Children have
this quality in abundance.*

If I were making up this game I would make it up
so that the foundation stone of existence would be
love, but not that stuff we are accustomed to calling
love — not emotional love. What I mean by "love" is
clarity of the Spirit or compassion. It doesn't want or
need fulfillment — it is fulfillment. It doesn't require
inspiration — it is inspiration. It never requires forgiveness — it is forgiveness. It is living, experientially,
in the shoes of all beings. It is, in a word, compassion.

The good news is that that is the way it is for all
beings . . . *and* the bad news is that there are barriers
to the experience and expression of that state of being.
Love sometimes comes disguised as hate and anger
and that is as bad as the news ever gets.

The context of transformation recognizes The
Truth that love is all there is and *comes from* That
Truth. Coming from The Truth of love requires nothing except being, and is actually the way it is with
people. It is a state of grace in which you know that

what is done by others in relationship to you carries a valuable contribution for your life, *no matter what it is.*

I have been carefully observing Houston for 16 months now. Never once have I seen him harm another being. Never once have I seen him interpret anyone's actions as harmful to him. Even when I lose it and yell at him, he recovers from his upset as soon as he expresses it, after which, play begins immediately *and the upset is over forever.* Houston does not carry grudges. He literally exists from the beingness of the other person and that presents itself as caring for other beings.

What I am telling you is that you were born with the context of transformation and you still have it operating inside the conditions of Scarcity, Inevitability, and Unworkability, inside a condition of insanity. That which passes for sanity includes the craziest things there are, like, for example the thought that one's life doesn't make a real difference, but more about that in another place.

These are matters you can't figure out. They just are, somewhat like gravity just is. The most basic abstractions are incomprehensible to the intellect, and love being all there is, is one of those abstractions. The most brilliant scientists in the world have no notion of what gravity is, it just is. In fact the phenomenon of gravity itself gives rise to notions and explanations. Gravity is, and you are a transformed being. If you think gravity isn't and you step off a tall building, you fall anyway. If you think you are not transformed, you are anyway, regardless of how you are acting.

In a hurry. Must get to the printer fast. There's the car, got to move.

"Byee!" A tiny voice sounds one of the 25 words it knows.

Where did that come from?

"Byee!" comes the voice from up above. The balcony over the driveway, of course!

Pressing his head between two rails, "Byee!"

Chapter 13

TRANSFORMATION

All children are special children.
The specialness comes from Who
They Are, not whose they are.

I have written about transformation in many places. However, nothing I can ever write expresses transformation as well as a child. Houston is a special child and he is by no means the only special child in the world. Any child could grace these pages and the result would be the same, for all children are special children. The special comes from Who They Are, not from whose they are.

People ask me frequently, "Just what is transformation?" The fact is that anything I can say is not it, and I usually say something anyway to wile away the time. The most accurate answer is that it is nothing — if you can think nothing for a moment it will transform your life for the rest of your life. Few of us ever think nothing, and the few who do think nothing, think nothing with great infrequency. We almost always think something, an example is the thought "I am thinking nothing" that is a something thought, that is, it is about a thought, namely the thought that you are thinking nothing.

You may ask where one can go to find someone thinking nothing. Go to your nearest young child, but you have to look fast, for those moments of nothing come and go very fast. When you know that all creation is ultimately from nothing, watching a child will be a full experience for you. As I write this, Houston is sitting in my lap marveling at the computer and pushing a random key now and then. He will settle for being no place else right now. He has no basis for experience with what he is seeing as the letters go on the screen and yet this little ball of fire sits transfixed watching the letters go on the screen — he is creating his experience from nothing.

You and I, almost all the time, create our experience from our concepts which are in turn based on experiences we have had in the past, the experience of which was based on experiences before that and on back to the original experiences which were based on nothing. With the accumulation of experiences and the organization of concepts to explain them, being truly alive becomes less and less likely.

That which allows human beings to call the way life is into being — language — is also that which prevents us from thinking nothing. We think in words in place of thinking from pure creation, pure nothing. The so-called geniuses of the world are simply those people who have retained the ability to create their thought from nothing, not even from words. The process Houston is engaged in while sitting at a computer, which he has no words or concepts to explain. is no different in nature than Einstein considering what happens to light as it passes a large mass, such as a star, and "seeing" that light, and thus space, is curved. One cannot reason one's way to such a conclusion and thus reasoning is revealed as a word-directed process that is contained in a closed system which excludes true creativity.

This obsession with words is the origin of our most debilitating feature as a species: our righteous beliefs and opinions. Words, which are creations, are held by the Mind as if they somehow existed in the universe before they were created by us. Words come so close to the beginning of life that we have difficulty knowing that they are creations which have themselves the power of creation. They are both a blessing and a curse, for when we create with words (which are themselves created from nothing) we forget that we are creating from nothing and begin to think that our creations have substance, that is we think we are creating from something.

The most advanced physicists of our times are now telling us that, as we observe the nature of "matter" more and more closely, it appears that matter is almost all space. The distance of an electron from its nucleus is equivalent to a ping-pong ball orbiting a basketball at several hundred miles distance. Not only that, an electron cannot be proven to exist, but is rather a postulate to explain certain phenomena. Matter now appears to physicists, not so much hard substance as a very complex *thought.*

I postulate this: you are the thinker who creates the universe around you — *literally,* and actually. And to make the game interesting, you blind yourself to that and play the part of another "thing" in the environment. Transformation, then, could be postulated to be the realization of the creation, while the creation is in process, that is during your lifetime, and the continuance of the creation, for no reason.

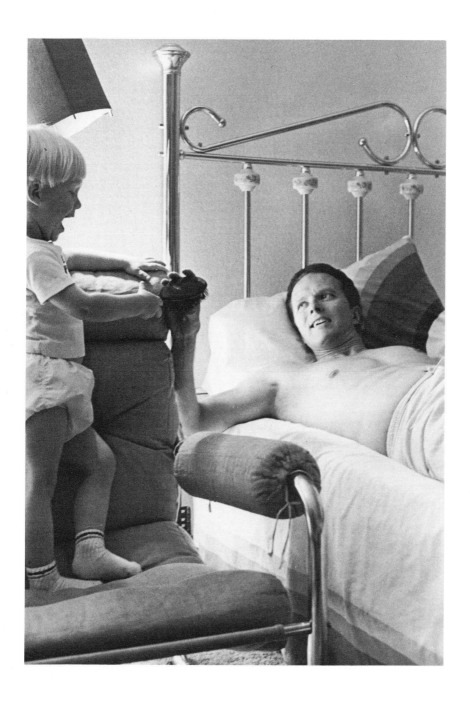

It's morning. Got to get up.

Here's Houston with my brush.

Here he is again with my wallet.

Here he comes again with my shoes.

It's morning. Got to get up.

Chapter 14

FREEDOM AND RESPONSIBILITY

*Children are born transformed,
yet their transformation has not yet
been earned.*

It is impossible for me to say if a child knows these things at birth. I suspect that the knowing is forgotten in the womb or perhaps as early as conception. Children, while demonstrating transformation in an incredibly free manner, nevertheless have not yet been challenged by the conditions of life and, in this sense, are not yet responsible for their own transformation. It is, in effect, a gift which has not yet been earned. Children therefore, could be said to have freedom, but at no responsibility.

The next step is the challenge by Satan — that is by the Conditions of Life: Scarcity, Inevitability, and Unworkability. Almost without fail, Satan wins, or said another way, one sells one's Spirit for survival by going into agreement with the Conditions and living life *from* the fundamental notions that things are scarce, inevitable, and do not work. One's predicament at this stage is *no* freedom and *no* responsibility. Life is a large heap of junk and you are just trying to get through it because you are afraid to die. At the bottom of this predicament is suicide when one decides death would be better if one were actually dead, rather than being one of the upright dead. No freedom and no responsibility is a stage one must traverse on the way to one's transformation and is, therefore, part of the transformation itself.

When you pass through this gate, life gets much worse very quickly. This is merely the Condition's response to transformation. Years may pass in a worsened condition. Then, as you begin to actually experience your transformation, the next event is that the people around you begin to hate and despise you. Once again the Condition asserts itself. It should be clear to you at this stage that the Condition is a spiritual entity which you create and which is thus infinitely smaller that Who You Actually Are.

This realization is your liberation into the realm of life from which you originally came: Freedom and Responsibility, or as I like to call it: Heaven on Earth (See the last chapter of TRANSFORMING #1).

So, to summarize the passages of transformation, they are:
(1) Freedom and Responsibility — prior to conception
(2) Freedom and No Responsibility — sometime between conception and birth until sometime in childhood
(3) No Freedom and No Responsibility — from sometime in childhood (the sellout) until the moment of transformation

(4) Responsibility, but still No Freedom — from the moment of choice (to transform oneself over and over again) to the time of liberation

(5) Freedom and Responsibility — from the time of liberation

I want to emphasize that before #4 (the choice), there is no hope of transformation. After the moment of choice, steps 1, 2, and 3 become themselves transformed. Transformation, therefore, has the power to reach into the past and transform that which was not transformed — the past is actually transformed. To say that another way: if one is on the path of transformation, all the stops along the way are, necessarily, transformed.

After #4, there will still be times of No Transformation (no freedom and no responsibility), and those times themselves become transformed as one chooses over and over again to transform oneself.

As I write these words in my home-office, I can hear Houston downstairs running back and forth, making clunking sounds on the floor with his little feet. One may legitimately ask: what is the point in this transformation business, and the answer is in the "clunk, clunk" of little feet. For, if there were no children in the world, I would soon forget Who I Am and revert to the Conditions of Life. You and I owe it to the children of the world, who are all our children, to transform ourselves.

Who do we think we are to live our lives in a selfish and destructive manner just because we like it that way?

Up in a high chair playing with his food. Vocal and effective with his demands.

Wants to be pulled over to the table, to be included in the meal.

Wants a glass of "Awa!" (agua - water - learning Spanish).

Clear that he deserves the best of treatment.

Also clear that others deserve the best of treatment as well.

Chapter 15

THE CHILDREN OF THE WORLD

*What do you say to the parent of
a child dying of hunger?*

Houston has never known hunger of the kind that fully one quarter of the children in the world know all too well, and if I have anything to say about it, he never will. That doesn't erase the fact that millions of our children are hungry right now.

When Houston cries out in hunger, it mobilizes me to feed him. It is an ingrained, automatic response - when he cries out I am on the way to get the food. If we are in a crowd of people, everyone in earshot is transfixed, in a sense, until that hunger is satisfied.

Houston is an incredible child, the kind of child you dream about having. He has a wonderful ability to comprehend his environment, to know what is going on around him, and his abilities will, of course, increase with age. If he should die, the loss to the world would be immeasureable . . . and do you know that there are millions of Houstons lost every year to starvation? Do you know that the parents of those children know intimately and profoundly the nature of the loss we all face without each one of those children who dies of hunger? I am not a unique parent in that regard.

What do you say to a child dying of hunger? How would you explain to that child's parents? Would you say that death was occurring because there is a scarcity of food in the world? Would you tell them that hunger and starvation are inevitable, that *someone* has to die and you are sorry that it is them or their children? Or how about "Nothing works anyway . . . if they didn't die of hunger, they would die from something else." Sounds ridiculous doesn't it? But, that is the kind of tripe rattling around in our heads because we have been hypnotized by the Conditions of Life. Would this junk satisfy you if your child were dying from hunger?

I want to take this opportunity to ask you to put yourself in touch with your commitment to the children of the world. The stand you take on such things makes a difference, and it makes a life or death difference to millions of children, especially. If you are not clear about the facts of hunger, read the section of TRANSFORMING #1 entitled The Persistence of Hunger in Our World. I know what Houston would say if we could somehow pose the question and he could answer, even though he doesn't talk yet. "Let's feed them!" It's a simple answer, one we adults are too smart to think of. I do not claim that the solutions to hunger will be easy, nor do I claim to have them in hand, nor do I think "feeding them!" is the entire answer. The fact is that people want the opportunity to be able to feed themselves and their children. However, the fact that we don't have the answers in hand is no excuse to not take the action that will first alleviate the problem and then reveal what needs to be done next.

If Houston, by being — simply being, can move you and me to take effective action on such an issue, imagine the contribution the children of the world have to make by living their lives and transforming their *being* into doing!! I am deeply moved by Houston's commitment and intended level of responsibility by having this book written at only 16 months of age. Who would have dared to be the source of such a book at such an age?

His new toy (a letter opener) taken away by Daddy.

A swat for Daddy, right on the leg!

No one, no matter how big, should just take something away from a person.

Daddy agrees, except for letter openers. And without the benefit of words, Houston understands.

Chapter 16

ABSOLUTE PARENTAL LOVE

Absolute love is the ground of be-
ing out of which all expressions
grow, both those expressions you
like and agree with and those you
don't like and don't agree with.

When I see Houston, I am always very aware of
seeing myself. I remember being a child and I still
carry that child within me, even though 40 years have
made their marks on my body (not many marks however). And when I look at Houston I almost always
remember my parents looking at me with such joy — I
couldn't understand it then. I do now.

No one has the opportunity to experience Who a
person is quite to the degree a parent has. When I look
into Houston's eyes, I am struck with awe, my heart
seems often to skip a beat, time for me stands still and
life goes on in successive moments of now that last for
eternity. In those moments out of time, when expression is impossible because time is standing still, I ap-
preciate the love my parents had for me more than I
can ever write. My parents, like all parents in their relationships with their children, loved me with an absolute love.

The absoluteness of parental love transcends, and makes unnecessary, and at the same stroke energizes and completes the actual expression, or evidence of love. We, as children, sometimes fail to notice absolute love in our search for the evidence to prove our parents loved us. Absolute love is the ground of being out of which the expression, or non-expression of love grows.

Some parents, out of their love for their children, do not show affection. They believe it is bad for children. That is a belief some people have, and those people love their children as much (absolutely) as another parent who showers his or her child with affection. Some parents leave their children to the care of other people and they do that out of the absoluteness of their love, believing, correctly or incorrectly, that it is in the best interest of the child.

So, if you are wondering if your parents really loved you, or if you really love your children — stop — they did, and you do. Absolute love is not something you have a choice about, it is that out of which choices are possible. It is even that out of which life itself is possible, and that includes all expressions, even hate. The truth is that hate is an expression of absolute love. The desire behind the emotion of hate is to contribute to the object of hate in such a way that the expression of absolute love, in which all emotions and non-emotions are grounded, can be more obvious.

If you are awake, you have noticed that what I am saying is that absolute love is the only thing in life that has no opposite. Emotional love has an opposite: hate or indifference, perhaps several opposites. Possessiveness has an opposite: charity. Attachment has an opposite: detachment. Conditional love has an opposite: unconditional love. Absolute love is that which gives rise to love, hate, possessiveness, charity, attachment, detachment, conditions and the absence of conditions.

This is the love that parents have for children, and it is a given, not something that you earn by acting "good" or coerce from someone by acting "bad."

When I look at Houston, God appears on earth in the face of a child. If you think I worship my son, you should understand that when I pick him up, God knows he can't get away, and that I am much, much stronger and smarter, for now, although I will not say wiser. Your parents love you like this and you love your children (all children) in this way. Absolute love is just the way it is.

Consider the plight of a parent who loves you absolutely and you think they are supposed to win a personality contest with you. And when this parent (or these parents) do not win your personality contest, you refuse to acknowledge their love — you go on a search to find out if your parents "really loved" you.

The problem with that is that you are failing to acknowledge what is, and when you fail to acknowledge something that is, it remains what is, anyway.

There is also another side of this coin, and that is the absolute love children have for their parents.

"Woof! Woof!" It's the Daddy dog coming for Houston on all fours.

"Woof! Woof!" and with a squeal of glee, Mr. Houston demonstrates his foot and leg speed.

The Daddy dog can't catch Mr. Houston.

Fathers will do anything for attention.

Chapter 17

THE ABSOLUTE LOVE CHILDREN HAVE FOR THEIR PARENTS

The ultimate teaching tool possessed by a child is a natural love which will not go away.

In relating to Houston I am most struck by the love he has for me. In fact, of all the facets of our relationships, this one stands out in the most dramatic relief. His love is a pure expression which puts all other expressions in the shade. This is the ultimate teaching tool possessed by a child.

We think we have to have something to teach in order to teach. Children have nothing to teach, and are thus the most powerful teachers on earth. You can learn more from a child about those things that mean the most to you in life than from any college professor, psychologist, theologian, psychiatrist, you name it.

Children teach by being, not be being full of information, which mercifully they are not, but just by simply being. To the extent that one is full of nothing, one can just simply be. And when one simply is, one is full of love. Thus children are full to the brim with love for their parents.

I don't have any changes to propose. In writing, I write from what is, not from what should be. Life, as it is, is perfect. Children, as they are, are perfect, and we are all children for all time.

Soft eyes, pug nose, cute little ears.

Playing in the kitchen with all the pots and pans on the floor.

Running through life. Thrilled with the adventure.

Awestruck with the gift of being alive.

Invitation

I invite you to correspond with me. You can reach me by
writing in care of:
CONTEXT PUBLICATIONS
20 LOMITA AVENUE
SAN FRANCISCO, CALIFORNIA 94122
U.S.A.